Classifying Reptiles

LOUISE AND RICHARD SPILSBURY

Heinemann
LIBRARY

www.heinemann.co.uk/library
Visit our website to find out more information about **Heinemann Library** books.

To order:
☎ Phone 44 (0) 1865 888066
🖹 Send a fax to 44 (0) 1865 314091
💻 Visit the Heinemann Bookshop at www.heinemann.co.uk/library to browse our catalogue and order online.

First published in Great Britain by Heinemann Library, Halley Court, Jordan Hill, Oxford OX2 8EJ, a division of Harcourt Education Ltd. Heinemann is a registered trademark of Harcourt Education Ltd.

Editorial: Jilly Attwood and Jennifer Tubbs
Design: Jo Hinton-Malivoire and AMR
Illustrations: David Woodroffe
Picture Research: Catherine Bevan, Hannah Taylor and Su Alexander
Production: Séverine Ribierre

Originated by Dot Gradations Ltd
Printed in Hong Kong, China by Wing King Tong

ISBN 0 431 16783 4
07 06 05 04 03
10 9 8 7 6 5 4 3 2 1

British Library Cataloguing in Publication Data
Spilsbury, Richard and Louise
Classifying Living Things – Reptiles
597.9'012
A full catalogue record for this book is available from the British Library.

Acknowledgements
For Harriet and Miles, slow-worm enthusiasts.

The publishers would like to thank the following for permission to reproduce photographs: Bruce Coleman: 5 (Joe McDonald), 13 (MPL Fogden), 16 (John Cancalosi), 18 (Kim Taylor), 20 (Jane Burton), 23 (Jim Watt), 29 (Alain Compost); Corbis: 24 (Peter Johnson); Nature Picture Library: 26; NHPA: 4 (Daniel Zupanc), 8 (Lady Philippa Scott), 9 (James Carmichael Jr), 14 (A.N.T.), 15 (Stephen Dalton), 19 (Norbert Wu), 25 (Daniel Heuclin), 27 (Eric Soder); Oxford Scientific Films: 6, 10 (Tui De Roy), 11 (Philippe Henry), 21, 12 (George Bryce), 17 (Brian Kennedy), 22 (Godfrey Merlen), 28 (Michael Fogden).

Cover photograph of Eyelash Viper babies reproduced with permission of Oxford Scientific Films.

Every effort has been made to contact copyright holders of any material reproduced in this book. Any omissions will be rectified in subsequent printings if notice is given to the publishers.

Contents

Words in the text in bold, **like this**, are explained in the Glossary.

How classification works

The Earth is populated with an immense variety of living things, from the largest whale to the tiniest insect. Scientists believe that all these **organisms** (living things) are the **descendants** of one group of simple organisms that lived millions of years ago.

Classification can help us to understand how different organisms might be related to each other. It also makes better sense of the great variety of organisms by sorting them into groups.

The body of a crocodile is one typical reptile shape. Other reptile groups such as snakes or turtles have different shapes.

Sorting life

Different living things are grouped according to the characteristics (features) that they have in common. Some are obvious at first glance. For example, any animal you see with feathers is a bird. There are many that are not so obvious, however. Fish, **mammals**, reptiles, birds and **amphibians** are classified together because they are all **vertebrates** (they have an internal backbone). Other less obvious characteristics used to classify organisms include how they **reproduce** (have babies), how they breathe and the type of skin they have.

There are many different ways to classify, and scientists often disagree about the best ways. Nevertheless, over time scientists have come up with a way of sorting all organisms.

From kingdoms to species

Living things are divided into huge groups called kingdoms. Plants, for example, are all grouped in one kingdom, and all animals are grouped in another. Each kingdom is made up of smaller groups, each called a **phylum**. A phylum contains several **classes**, classes contain **orders**, orders contain **families**, families contain **genera** (singular genus) and genera contain **species**. A species is a single kind of organism, such as a marine (sea-living) iguana.

Common and scientific names

Many living things have a common name. Common names such as 'iguana' are not always exact. For instance, there are two similar-looking types of iguana that live on the Galapagos islands – one feeds on land plants and one on seaweed.

To distinguish between similar organisms, scientists give every species a two-part name. The first name is that of the genus the organism belongs to. The second is the name of the species within that genus.

Using scientific names, it is easy to tell the two types of iguana apart. The land iguana has the name *Conolophus subcristatus* and the marine iguana is *Amblyrhynchus cristatus*.

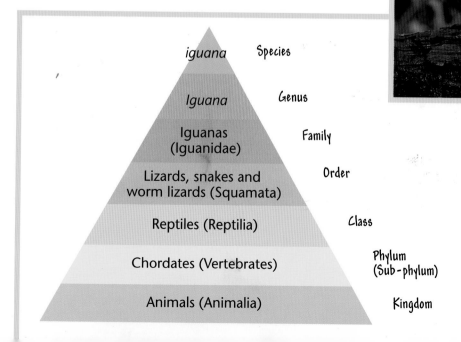

iguana	Species
Iguana	Genus
Iguanas (Iguanidae)	Family
Lizards, snakes and worm lizards (Squamata)	Order
Reptiles (Reptilia)	Class
Chordates (Vertebrates)	Phylum (Sub-phylum)
Animals (Animalia)	Kingdom

This pyramid shows the full classification for the common tree iguana – Iguana iguana.

What is a reptile?

Reptiles come in many shapes, sizes and colours, from giant armoured crocodiles and tortoises to brightly coloured lizards and snakes. However different reptiles look, they all share a number of characteristics that distinguish them from other types of animals:

- they are **vertebrates**
- their skin is covered by hard, protective **scales**
- they **reproduce** using eggs, which they lay on land
- they breathe oxygen (a gas in the air) using lungs
- they are **cold-blooded** – they cannot control their own body temperature so their bodies are always as hot or cold as their surroundings.

Types of reptiles

Reptiles are classified by their body structure – both inside and out. The main reptile groups are lizards, snakes, turtles and crocodiles. Lizards usually have four limbs, long bodies and tails. Snakes always have no limbs. Turtles and tortoises have a bony shell covering their backs. Crocodiles look a bit like lizards but with long, toothed jaws and heavily armoured skin.

There are two other groups of reptiles. The first, contains only one **species**, the tuatara, which looks like a lizard. Members of the other group – the amphisbaenids or worm lizards – look rather like snakes. These groups are classified separately as they have different skeletons to other reptiles.

It is clear that snakes are vertebrates if we look at their skeletons.

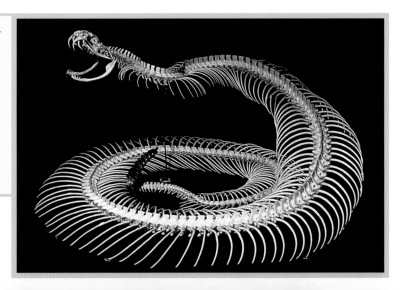

This table shows the orders of reptiles and gives some examples of main families and species.

Order	Suborder	Families	No. of species	Examples
Squamata (lizards, snakes and amphisbaenids)	Lizards (Sauria)	Agamids (Agamidae)	300	Frilled dragon
		Anguids (Anguidae)	75	Slow-worm
		Beaded lizards (Helodermatidae)	2	Gila monster
		Chameleons (Chamaeleonidae)	85	Jackson's chameleon
		Geckos (Gekkonidae)	800	Leopard gecko
		Iguanas (Iguanidae)	650	Green iguana
		Lacertids (Lacertidae)	200	Viviparous lizard
		Monitors (Varanidae)	31	Komodo dragon
		Skinks (Scincidae)	1275	Blue-tailed skink
	Snakes (Serpentes)	Boas and pythons (Boidae)	60	Anaconda, tree python
		Rear-fangs (Colubridae)	1500	Garter snake
		Cobras (Elapidae)	170	Indian cobra
		Sea snakes (Hydrophiidae)	50	Dusky sea snake
		Blind snakes (Typhlopidae)	200	Southern blind snake
		Vipers (Viperidae)	180	Diamondback rattlesnake
Rynchocephalia (tuatara)		(Sphenodontidae)	2	Northern tuatara
Crocodilia (crocodiles, alligators and caimans)		Alligators (Alligatoridae)	8	American alligator
		Crocodiles (Crocodylidae)	14	Nile crocodile
		Gavial (Gavialidae)	1	Gharial
Chelonia (reptiles with shells)	Turtles, tortoises and terrapins (Cryptodira)	Marine turtles (Cheloniidae)	5	Hawksbill turtle
		Snapping turtles (Chelydridae)	2	Alligator snapper
		Freshwater turtles (Emydidae)	76	Diamondback terrapin
		Tortoises (Testudinidae)	40	Giant tortoise
		Soft-shell turtles (Trionychidae)	20	Florida soft-shell turtle
	Side-necked Turtles (Pleurodira)	Snake-necks (Chelidae)	21	Matamata
		Side-necks (Pelomedusidae)	14	Twist-necked turtle

Skin and bone

Reptiles live all over the world except in cold deserts. Many live successfully in hot desert conditions. Their skin is an important key to survival in such extreme conditions.

Reptile skin is dry and covered in **scales**. Scales are thick pieces of dead skin. Not all scales are the same. Scales can be as tough as the strong crests on crocodile backs but as delicate as the smooth scales of a corn snake.

Out with the old

Lizards and snakes shed (discard and replace) their skin regularly when it gets old or worn. The skin of tortoises and crocodiles just gets thicker with larger scales as they grow.

Dry and warm

All scaly skin is tough enough to help protect reptiles' soft insides. It is also waterproof. This helps stop water inside reptiles being lost through evaporation (changing into water vapour), allowing them to live in dry places.

Scaly skin may keep water in, but it loses heat easily. As they are **cold-blooded**, reptiles need to **bask** (remain still and warm up) to get enough energy to move. Crocodiles bask on warm riverbanks, some lizards stand with their sides facing the sun, and snakes may coil up on warm earth. As with other animals, too much heat can damage a reptile's body. In very hot **habitats** reptiles usually hide from the sun during the day.

Marine iguanas stand up to soak up energy from the sun after swimming in the cold sea.

Vertebrate variations

The name 'reptile' comes from the Latin word *repere*, which means crawling. Not all reptiles crawl, though. Reptiles have different-shaped skeletons because they live in many different ways.

Like all **vertebrates**, reptiles have a tough but flexible internal backbone. The backbone supports the body. It is connected to other bones such as ribs, which protect **organs** such as the heart from damage. Turtles have an outer shield of horn (a shell) covering a dome of plate-shaped ribs connected to the backbone. This forms a protective box around their bodies.

The scales on this pit viper's body are different sizes. Tough scales help protect the front of its head as it moves and catches food.

The backbone is also connected to limbs for movement. Lizards and crocodiles have four short, angled legs that carry their body just above the ground. Snakes move without legs. They have very flexible backbones connected to as many as 400 ribs. They slither along, twisting their bodies to and fro using strong muscles.

Most reptiles have teeth. Crocodiles have a mouthful but some snakes have just a few inside their throats for gripping onto food as they swallow it. Turtles have no teeth but use their jagged jaw bones for biting. Reptiles have no chewing teeth so they either swallow food whole or rip chunks off.

Reptile reproduction

Reptiles **reproduce** on land by laying eggs. One of the biggest dangers for all young animals developing inside eggs on land is drying out. To prevent this, all reptiles eggs have a tiny puddle of fluid inside them.

Reptile eggs

Reptile eggs come in different shapes and sizes. Some are shaped like big jelly beans, others like ping-pong balls or even like knobbly carrots. Most reptile eggs are surrounded by a soft, leathery skin, but some, such as gecko eggs, have a hard shell a bit like that of birds' eggs. Inside each egg is a special but delicate skin that the baby can breathe through, a bag of watery fluid and a yolk (food) for the developing reptile. Reptile eggs are more delicate than birds' eggs. If you turn a turtle egg over, for example, the baby turtle inside will probably suffocate and die because the special skin can easily get damaged.

Sea turtles return to the same warm beaches each year to lay their eggs. They dig holes with their legs and lay hundreds of eggs deep in the sand.

Incubation and hatching

Reptile babies can only develop properly and hatch if their eggs stay at the right temperature. This is called **incubation**. Parent reptiles have different ways of making sure the eggs are warm enough. Alligators living by cool, shady riverbanks lay their eggs in mounds of leaves, which produce warmth as they rot. Pythons coil around their eggs and shiver their muscles to keep them warm.

Covering eggs to incubate them also hides them from **predators** such as egg-eating birds. Most female reptiles abandon their eggs once they are laid. Some, such as alligators, guard their eggs until they hatch. When reptiles hatch they look like tiny versions of their parents and most can look after themselves straight away.

Internal incubation

Some **species** of reptiles, such as pit vipers, incubate and hatch their eggs inside their bodies. Although this means the eggs have more protection, it also means these reptiles have fewer eggs because there is not much room inside!

Young alligators, like many other reptiles, have a special egg tooth on their upper jaw that they use to cut their way out of their tough shell when they hatch.

Skinks, geckos and other lizards

Lizards (**order** Squamata, suborder Sauria) are the largest group of reptiles. They have distinct necks and tails, ear openings behind their eyes, and usually four legs. Although many lizards look a bit like crocodiles on the outside, they are similar to snakes on the inside. For example, like snakes they have sensitive pits in their mouths called Jacobson's organ, which they use to taste with. Lizards are therefore classified in the same order as snakes. Lizards, though, have fewer bones in their skulls than snakes.

The largest family

The skink **family** (Scincidae) contains the largest number of **species** of all lizard families. Skinks are 15 to 30 centimetres long usually and live all around the world, usually on the ground or hidden in burrows. They are grouped together because they have no obvious neck, and have smooth skin covered with shiny rounded **scales**, broad tongues, scaly eyelids and (usually) very small legs.

Sand skinks live in hot desert **habitats**. They 'swim' just below the surface of the sand by wriggling their bodies from side to side. This is an easier way of getting around on shifting ground than walking on legs and toes.

The tails of many lizards break off easily so they can escape from predators that have grabbed them. A new tail then grows. This skink has a blue tail to make sure predators go for its tail rather than its delicate head.

Sticking around

Geckos (family Gekkonidae) are small climbing lizards that live in warm parts of the world. They are grouped together because they have toes **adapted** for climbing and no scales on their heads. Many geckos have no eyelids – they clean their eyes by licking them.

Geckos are mainly **nocturnal** and catch and eat insects. They are very noisy, usually making repeated calls to let other geckos know where they are. When they are frightened, the screech of baby leopard geckos sounds like air leaving the stretched end of a balloon.

Legless lizards

Several lizard families have no legs. This is an adaptation that helps them move through the thick grass and loose earth they live in. Despite their name, slow-worms (family Anguidae) are lizards not worms – they have scaly bodies, hard skulls and eyes with lids.

All alone

The tuatara lives on islands off New Zealand. It looks like a lizard but is classified in a group on its own partly because of the number of holes in its skull and the positioning of its teeth.

Gecko toes have ridged, bristle-covered pads and sharp claws, which makes it easy for geckos to climb, even on smooth surfaces such as glass.

Slow-worms are most active at dusk. They hunt slow-moving prey such as slugs and worms.

Iguana and monitor groups

The iguana group contains iguanas, agamids and chameleons. These are all lizards with heavy bodies, short necks, fleshy tongues and numerous belly **scales**. The other major group of lizards is the monitor group, which includes monitor lizards and beaded lizards. They have tiny, knobbly scales on their backs and forked tongues.

Iguanas and agamids

Iguanas (**family** Iguanidae) are generally large lizards that live on land, up trees and even in the sea, in North, Central and South America. Many male iguanas have crests and brightly coloured throat fans that they display (show others) to attract females or to warn other males to stay away. Rhinoceros iguanas have thick scales like horns on their heads and a heavy build to avoid being damaged in fights.

This frilled dragon is warning other animals to get away. It does this by spreading its frill, hissing and moving forward.

Agamids (family Agamidae) live in different parts of the world to iguanas. One **species** called frilled dragons run away fast on their back legs when they see a possible **predator**. If cornered, they stretch open a frill of skin around their neck using special **cartilage** struts by their throat. The moloch – or thorny devil – is covered with thorn-like scales to put off predators. If it is frightened it tucks its head in to become a prickly ball.

Hidden hunters

Chameleons (family Chameleonidae) look very different to iguanas and agamids because of their special **adaptations** for life in trees hunting for insect **prey**. They have a long sticky tongue, eyes that can swivel in different directions, a prehensile (gripping) tail and long legs with joined toes shaped like tongs that they use to grip branches. Chameleons have **camouflaged** skin – it changes colour if they move on to a different background. It also changes colour with its mood – an angry chameleon goes black with rage.

A chameleon swivels its eyes in different directions to watch out for insect prey. When it has spotted a meal it moves closer to catch it by catapulting out its tongue.

The monitor group

Monitor lizards (family Varanidae) have long heads, sharp claws and can swim well. They are sometimes massive – the Komodo dragon is a monitor that can reach 3 metres in length. It hides in dense forest on certain Indonesian islands waiting to ambush prey such as wild boar and deer.

The gila monster and the beaded lizard (family Helodermatidae) live in hot deserts and are the only two poisonous lizards. Their backs have striking patterns of black, pink or yellow scales. These markings warn other animals to keep away. If attacked, they bite and grip on while strong poison runs along grooves in their teeth into their victim.

Non-venomous snakes

Snakes are classified in the same **order** (Squamata) as lizards because they have similar skeletons. They are grouped in a different suborder (Serpentes) from lizards because all snakes are different from lizards in several ways.

What are snakes?

Snakes have no legs, long bodies and short tails. They have no ear openings – instead of hearing, they sense movements around them, feeling vibrations through the ground. Instead of moveable eyelids they have transparent **scales** to protect their eyes. All snakes are carnivores (meat-eaters). Their jaws are flexible and loosely connected to their skull so they can open their mouths wide – and even dislocate (unhinge) their lower jaws – to eat large **prey**.

Snakes can be divided into those that inject venom (poison) into their prey and those that do not. Rear-fangs, pythons and burrowers do not inject venom.

The king snake is a rear-fang snake that eats prey ranging from frogs to rattlesnakes.

Rear-fangs

Rear-fangs are the largest snake **family** (Colubridae). They live around the world and include king snakes, corn and garter snakes. They get their name because of the large teeth at the back of their jaws that most use to grip on to prey as they swallow it. Some rear-fangs use their fangs to slit open eggs they have eaten so they can swallow the contents. A few rear-fangs produce weakly venomous saliva but they cannot inject it.

In the loop

Boas and pythons (family Boidae) include the largest snakes in the world, such as the anaconda of South America (up to 10 metres long) and the reticulated python of Asia. Some of the reasons they are grouped together are their large belly scales, obvious necks and flexible upper jaw. Most live in trees, gripping on to branches with their belly scales, but some, like the anaconda, live mostly in water.

Boas and pythons kill large prey – usually **mammals** ranging from rats to deer – by squeezing them to death. This is called constriction. They bite and crush smaller prey in their jaws.

Burrowers

Some families of snakes are grouped together because they are **adapted** for burrowing. Blind snakes (family Typhlopidae) have thin, worm-like bodies. They use their hard, blunt head to push through soil, getting a grip using a sharp spine on their tail. They have tiny eyes as they live in dark burrows and find their prey – mainly ants – using their sense of smell. Their scales protect them from ant bites, but some also produce bad smells that repel ants.

Constrictors catch their prey using sharp teeth and then coil their strong body around it to stop it breathing.

Venomous snakes

Cobras, vipers and sea snakes inject venom to paralyse (stop movement) or kill their **prey**. They may also threaten to use venom as a defence if a **predator** tries to attack them. When a snake is close enough to its prey it strikes by jabbing its fangs into the target and injecting venom. It then pulls its fangs away quickly, as they are fragile and might be damaged. Only when the poison has worked will it swallow its prey. Venomous snakes can be classified by the type of teeth they have.

Cobras – fixed fangs

The cobra group (**family** Elapidae) includes snakes such as the king cobra, krait, taipan and mamba. They are grouped together because their fangs are fixed in position in their upper jaw. Fixed fang snakes are mostly **nocturnal** hunters. Their venom moves down grooves in the fangs into the prey once they have bitten it. Fixed fang snakes mostly feed on rats, lizards and frogs.

Rattlesnakes are pit vipers that get their name from the loosely connected segments at the tip of their tail. The snake shakes its tail in defence, making a noise to ward off other creatures. For attack it has long folding fangs.

Vipers – folding fangs

Snakes in the family Viperidae are classified together because their long, curved fangs are hollow, connected to their venom **glands**, and fold into their mouths. When vipers strike, they fold their fangs down and large muscles at the back of their diamond-shaped heads pump venom through the fangs into their victim. When not in use, fangs fold up into grooves in their mouths for protection.

Vipers usually ambush their prey. Pit vipers have special pits (holes) on their heads that they use to detect heat given off by **mammals** such as mice when they approach. Young copperheads hide in leaf litter and waggle their yellow tail tip so it resembles a worm. They do this to attract worm-eating prey such as frogs.

Sea snakes

One group of snakes is **adapted** for life in shallow **tropical** seawater. Members of the family Hydrophiidae have flattened tails for swimming. They come to the surface to breathe air into their lungs, close valves over their nostrils and dive for up to five hours. Sea snake venom is generally stronger than other snake venom, so they can paralyse their slippery fish prey quickly before it gets away.

Lethal cocktail

Venom is special spit made in large venom glands in the snake's head. It contains a mixture of chemicals. Some chemicals paralyse or kill the prey but others digest (break down) the prey from the inside.

Sea snakes hunt in holes in coral reefs for fish prey such as eels.

Turtles in freshwater habitats

Turtles are amongst the easiest to recognize of all reptiles. All turtles (**order** Testudines) have shortened bodies covered by a rigid, box-shaped **carapace** (shell). The carapace is a layer of hard, large **scales** covering flat, arched rib bones, which are attached to the backbone. Many turtles also have a tough shell under their belly called a **plastron**.

Turtles have no teeth although many can bite well. Their jaws are often beak-like and have sharp edges. Most turtles live in shallow freshwater and can hold their breath underwater. Their legs are **adapted** for swimming – either by having a broad, flattened shape (flippers), or by having webbed toes.

Pond turtles

Freshwater turtles (**family** Emydidae) group together about a third of all turtle **species**, such as terrapins, painted, bog and wood turtles. They live in pond, marsh or estuary **habitats** in Asia and North, South and Central America. All have hard, domed shells and eat insects, snails and fish. Box turtles pull in their head, legs and tail, and raise their plastron to meet their carapace to form a tight protective box if attacked by a hopeful **predator**.

Freshwater turtles, such as this red-eared terrapin, have stout legs with webbed toes for life both on land and in water.

Fearsome turtles

Snapping turtles (family Chelydridae) have very sharp jaws and a thick, ridged shell, which is often covered with growing pondweed. The alligator snapper of southern USA can weigh 90 kilograms. It has a muscular, worm-like growth on its tongue that it waggles to lure inquisitive prey such as fish, frogs or other turtles. Snapping turtles also eat water plants and floating fruit.

A softer side

Softshell turtles (family Trionychidae) have flat, smooth carapaces covered with leathery skin instead of scales. They live in rivers, streams and wetlands. Soft shells provide less protection than hard shells, but are lighter to carry around. Many, such as the Chinese softshell, have long necks and noses that they use like snorkels so they can breathe while remaining mostly hidden underwater.

Side-necked turtles

Most turtles pull their necks straight back under their carapace for protection. They are classified together in the suborder Cryptodira. Side-necked turtles such as the matamata are classified in a separate group (suborder Pleurodira) because they pull in their necks by folding them sideways.

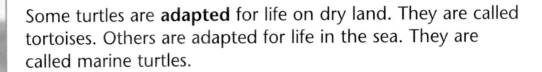

Some turtles are **adapted** for life on dry land. They are called tortoises. Others are adapted for life in the sea. They are called marine turtles.

Tortoises

Tortoises (**family** Testudinidae) have stubby heads and high, dome-shaped **carapaces** covered with large **scales**. Their feet are shaped like clubs for walking and have long heavy claws for digging in hard ground.

Most are herbivores – they feed on plants. Garden tortoises avoid cold seasons by burrowing into leaves and hibernating (sleeping through winter) until it is warm again. Desert tortoises dig burrows up to 12 metres long and return to them to shelter from hot weather. Giant tortoises live on various oceanic islands. The Galapagos Islands in the Pacific Ocean were named after the Spanish word for the giant tortoises (*galapago*) found there. Giant tortoises may reach lengths of over 1 metre, weigh over 225 kilograms and live for 100 years. They like to cool down in muddy ponds when it is hot.

Some Galapagos giant tortoises like this one are called saddlebacks as their carapaces arch like saddles. This allows them to stretch their necks to eat taller plants.

Marine turtles

Two families of large turtles live almost their whole lives at sea. Most marine turtles, such as the green turtle or olive ridley sea turtle, have hard, smooth carapaces and are classified in the family Cheloniidae. The leatherback turtle (family Dermochelyidae) is classified separately, as its ridged carapace is covered with **cartilage** rather like leathery skin instead of scales. It can reach nearly 3 metres in length and a weight of over 500 kilograms. It swims over large areas of open ocean, feeding on slow-moving **prey** such as jellyfish, which it grips on to using its jagged beak-like jaws and the spines inside its throat.

Marine turtles often migrate (regularly travel) very long distances to lay their eggs on land. The female green sea turtle may live for 30 years until she is ready to lay eggs. She then migrates up to 2000 kilometres to the same beach where she hatched out of an egg, finding her way by sensing magnetic forces in the Earth – a bit like having an inbuilt compass. She then drags herself on to the beach, digs a hole with her back legs and lays over 200 eggs. Just a few will survive and grow up to return to the same beach in future to lay their own eggs.

True crocodiles and gharials

Crocodiles are massive, heavily armoured reptiles grouped in the **order** Crocodilia. There are 23 **species** in the world, including true crocodiles, gharials, alligators and caimans. Most live in **tropical** rivers and lakes.

All species of crocodile have bodies, heads and tails that are long and legs that are short. Their thick **scales** are strengthened with bony plates for protection. Some scales are smooth and flat, others form hard ridges on their backs and tails. Like other reptiles, crocodiles absorb energy from the sun's warmth through their scales when they **bask** on riverbanks.

Catching food

Crocodiles usually hunt prey such as fish in the water, although they also catch food on land. Crocodiles have eyes and nostrils on top of their heads, so they can see and breathe while keeping their body and the rest of their head hidden underwater. Their long jaws contain at least 60 heavy teeth. Crocodiles have a special flap behind their tongues to stop them drowning when they open their mouths to catch food underwater. They produce strong stomach juices and swallow stones to help them break food down rapidly. The stones also help them stay submerged underwater.

Crocodiles use their long, muscular tails for swimming rather than their webbed hind feet. This crocodile is sliding into the water after basking in the sun.

True crocodiles

True crocodiles have long and tapering jaws. The fourth tooth from the front of the lower jaw can be seen clearly when their jaws are closed. Members of this **family** (Crocodylidae) live mostly in freshwater but the saltwater crocodile swims in the sea between the islands where it lives. The largest, the Indopacific crocodile, can reach up to 7 metres in length.

Large crocodiles often catch big **mammals** or birds by surprise. Nile crocodiles wait, hidden, for wildebeest and even lions to come for a drink at a waterhole. They then lunge out of the water, grabbing their prey and pulling it into the water to drown it. They lodge the prey between rocks or tree roots to stop it moving, grip on with their teeth, and then rotate their whole body to rip bits off to swallow.

Gharials

The gharial (family Gavialidae), which lives in rivers in India and Nepal, is classified separately from true crocodiles as it has very long, narrow jaws **adapted** to trap its prey – fast-moving, slippery fish. Males have a bulbous end to their snouts, which they use to make their calls louder when they call females during the **mating** season.

Gharials have lots of curved, sharp interlocking teeth to catch fish with.

Alligators and caimans

Alligators and caimans (**family** Alligatoridae) are classified separately to crocodiles although they appear to be very similar. The differences are that their jaws are broader and shorter and the upper jaw overlaps the lower jaw when their mouths are closed. Also, on each side of an alligator's lower jaw, the fourth tooth fits into a socket on the upper jaw.

Alligator breeding

Alligators are unusual amongst crocodiles in the care they give to their young. After a female alligator has **mated**, she builds a nest out of plants and mud on a riverbank above the water. She lays about 50 eggs in the nest and covers them over carefully. She then stays on guard nearby for around two months as they **incubate**. She does this because many animals, such as monitor lizards and racoons, like to eat her eggs.

When the babies hatch they call out and the mother breaks open the nest. She even helps crack some of her eggs open so the babies hatch more easily. The babies stay together in a group and their mother guards them for up to two years until they are big enough to look after themselves.

*The female American alligator is very protective of her young. They will often **bask** in safety on her back or head.*

The spectacled caiman gets its name from the bony ridge connecting its eyes which looks a bit like spectacles. Females often share a nest, and share the task of looking after each other's babies after the eggs hatch.

Caimans

Caimans are close relatives of alligators but they live in different parts of the world. Caimans live in South American rivers such as the Amazon. They have short skulls, often with ridges down them, and bony overlapping **scales** on their bellies.

Dwarf caimans only grow about 1.5 metres long – less than any other in the crocodile **order**. They have short upturned snouts that they use to dig burrows to shelter in during the day. They are **nocturnal** hunters of crabs in the water but also beetles and other insects on land.

Ancient survivors

Ancestors of today's crocodiles first lived on Earth when dinosaurs were alive. **Fossil** bones suggest some looked like crocodiles of today but bigger and that others looked a bit different – one even had hooves!

Larger caimans eat mostly fish, such as piranhas and catfish, and frogs. They can even leap out of the water to catch waterbirds. The black caiman – which can grow up to 6 metres – catches larger **prey** such as a sort of giant rodent called a capybara.

Reptiles all over

Reptiles come in a great variety of shapes and sizes and have very different ways of life. Reptiles that look as different as tortoises and rattlesnakes are easy to classify separately. They look different because they have different **adaptations** to life. For example, a tortoise's **carapace** – which makes it look a bit like a walking box – is an adaptation it uses for protection.

Sidewinders are adapted to the desert habitat they live in. They move like this to keep as much of their body off the burning hot sand as possible.

Same solution

Just to confuse things, other reptiles classified in different orders can look very similar because they have similar **adaptations**. For example, burrowing lizards, burrowing snakes and worm lizards are similar in that they have no limbs and strong heads for pushing and wriggling through holes in the soil, but they belong to separate **orders**.

Worm, lizard or snake?

Worm lizards look like big worms. They are long and thin, live mostly in the soil, and often have rings of scales around their bodies like the rings around worms. They are actually related to both lizards and snakes – they have scales and they are **vertebrates**, for example – but are classified in a group all of their own because of their different skeletons.

Classifying characteristics

Other animals may share many reptile characteristics but are classified separately because they do not share them all. For example, salamanders are vertebrates, reproduce using eggs, breathe partly through their lungs and are **cold-blooded**. But they are classified as **amphibians**, not reptiles, because their moist skin is not covered in **scales** and they breathe through their skin as well as their lungs.

Many reptiles appear to be exceptions to the rules. Some, such as shingleback skinks and garter snakes, give birth to live young. In fact, they reproduce using eggs. Their babies develop within transparent egg skins inside their mother and most hatch out just after they emerge from their mother.

Classification can be difficult when characteristics overlap or are difficult to spot. The most important thing about reptile classification is the way it can help us learn more about the fantastic variety of reptiles around the world.

A brief history of reptiles

Reptiles are thought to have amphibian **ancestors**. The first reptiles appeared on Earth over 300 million years ago. Unlike amphibians, reptiles laid eggs with protective shells and a water supply inside for their developing babies. They also had thicker skins with scales, which helped them live in warmer, drier **habitats**.

The Komodo dragon has a special characteristic – jagged teeth. They are doubly effective for both gripping prey and making sure any bitten prey that escape die from blood poisoning.

Glossary

adaptation special features that help living things to survive in their habitat

amphibian class of animals, e.g. a newt

ancestor relative in the past, like a grandparent

bask get warm in the sun

camouflage colour, shape or pattern that disguises an animal against its background

carapace hard shell

cartilage bendy skeleton material

class classification grouping. Each class is divided into orders.

cold-blooded term describing animals that cannot control their own body temperature the way warm-blooded animals can, so they are always as hot or cold as their surroundings

descendant later generation of an organism, like a grandchild

digest break down food for use by the body

family classification grouping. Vipers are a family of snakes.

fossil remains of organisms that once lived on Earth

genus (plural **genera**) classification grouping. Each genus is divided into species.

gland place in an animal's body that secretes particular fluids

habitat place where organisms live

incubation keeping eggs at the right temperature for the babies to develop

mammal class of animals. Mammals are warm-blooded and usually hairy. Their babies grow inside the mother, who suckles them and cares for them after they are born.

mate when a male fertilizes a female so that her eggs start to develop into babies

nocturnal active at night

order classification grouping. There are four orders within the class of reptile.

organ part of the body with a specific job to do, such as the liver or heart

organism living thing

phylum (plural **phyla**) classification grouping. Each phylum is divided into classes.

plastron lower shell of a turtle

predator animal that hunts and eats other animals

prey animal hunted and eaten by another animal

reproduce have babies

scales overlapping or interlocking pieces that form a protective layer over reptile skin

species classification grouping. A green iguana is a species of iguana.

tropical living in parts of the world near the equator (tropics)

vertebrates animals with internal skeleton of bone or cartilage

Further resources

Books

DK Eyewitness Guides: Reptiles, Colin McCarthy (Dorling Kindersley, 2000)

Keeping Unusual Pets: Geckos, Sonia Hernandez-Divers (Heinemann Library, 2002)

Keeping Unusual Pets: Snakes, June McNicholas (Heinemann Library, 2002)

Life Processes: Classification, Holly Wallace (Heinemann Library, 2000)

Websites

www.bristolzoo.org.uk/fact/index.html
   Look at fact sheets for different reptiles.
www.nps.gov/ever/eco/gator.htm
   Find out about alligators in the Everglades National Park.
www.reptilepark.com.au/animals/reptiles/Index.html
   From snakes to skinks, learn where they like to live, what they eat and how they behave.

Index